A Little Drink of Water

A Devotional of Spiritual Awakening

Kathy,
May the words within this book
comfort you give you strength &
encouragement.
Love,
D

Dianna Caraballo

Halo Publishing International

Copyright © 2015 Dianna Caraballo
All rights reserved.

No part of this book may be reproduced in any manner without the written consent of the publisher except for brief excerpts in critical reviews or articles.

ISBN: 978-1-61244-325-6
Library of Congress Control Number: 2014918905

Printed in the United States of America

Published by Halo Publishing International
1100 NW Loop 410
Suite 700 - 176
San Antonio, Texas 78213
Toll Free 1-877-705-9647
Website: www.halopublishing.com
E-mail: contact@halopublishing.com

I dedicate this book to my granddaughter, Sophia. Her presence has brought peace, joy, and new hope, into my life and everyone around her. She is her Mimi's daily drink of water.

I also want to thank all my family and friends that continue to encourage, support and inspire me to write and share the gift that God has given me.

Special thanks to my son, Adam for editing my words, and to my daughter, Ericka who continuously pushed me to write. Without you two, this book would not have happened. Much love to you both.

CONTENTS

THE NAME ABOVE ALL NAMES	7
A LISTENING HEART	9
SPEAK A BLESSING	11
MAKE ME-OVER	13
FAITH THAT CONQUERS FEAR	15
SEE WITH YOUR HEART NOT YOUR EYES	17
NO WORRIES	19
FROZEN IN TIME	21
THE KINGDOM AWAITS	23
TELL YOUR STORY	25
SHARING WORDS OF LOVE	27
FIRST IMPRESSIONS	29
CHIRST-LIKE	31
ROLE MODEL	33
WHAT'S IN YOUR ALABASTER BOX?	35
HERE WE GO AGAIN...	37
SPIRITUAL EYES	39
WE ARE WONDERFULLY MADE	40
VALLEY OF INDECISION	42
THROUGH THE STORM	44
NO GIANT IS TOO TALL	46
I CHOOSE	49
DO YOU BELIEVE?	51
I HEAR VOICES	53
FREE INDEED	55

HIDE ME O LORD	57
TOUCH SOMEONE	59
WHOSE MIND IS IT ANYWAY	61
YOUR CRIES NEVER FALL ON A DEAF EAR	63
WINDOWS TO THE SOUL	65
LET YOUR TESTIMONY SPEAK FOR YOU	67
YOU TALKIN` TO ME...	69
SWEET GIFT OF GOD	71
MANIFESTATIONS OF GOD'S AGAPE LOVE	73
ARE YOU A BRANCH, A LEAF, OR THE TRUNK	75
I WAS SENT TO HELP YOU	77
MORNING THOUGHTS	79
MAKE IT A SPIRITUAL DAY	81
LIFE TO REMEMBER	83
MY SON... THE SAILOR	85
I HAVE A FRIEND	87
A MOTHER'S LOVE	89
THINKING OUT LOUD QUOTES	92

THE NAME ABOVE ALL NAMES

When I was growing up I used to pretend that I had a different name. I would say that my name was Cassey, or Rachel. I even remember saying once that it was Princess Dianna. Maybe that is the reason that I was so enamored with Princess Diana when she married Prince Charles. Yes, I am smiling to myself.

I did not like my name and wanted to change it. It is amazing to me that as I grew up I found out that I was not alone in my disdain for what I thought was not a "cool enough" name, and many others felt the same as I did. Our birth name; given to us by our parents. I learned to live with it and researched the origin of the name, root and spiritual meaning of it. In my quest to learn the meaning of my name I have to admit I started to like the name that was chosen for me. I think I will keep it.

I want to talk about another name. A name that is so diverse it can mean virtually anything you want it to mean. The name that I am referring to is God. Here are just a few meanings of His name:

EL, ELOAH: God "mighty, strong, prominent." ELOHIM: God "Creator, Mighty and Strong."

ADONAI: "Lord." YHWH / YAHWEH / JEHOVAH: "LORD." YAHWEH-JIREH: "The Lord Will Provide." YAHWEH-RAPHA: "The Lord Who Heals." YAHWEH-SHALOM: "The Lord Our Peace." EL-GIBHOR: "Mighty God." JESUS, "God saves."

These are just a few of the names pinned in the Bible for the one true God. The beautiful aspect of the fact that God has so many names is to simply say He is the God of everything! His name, in whatever form you use it can accomplish anything that you need. That is powerful in its-own right.

Thought for the day: Your name has a meaning. If you have not already done so, why not search it out and see where it came from, what it means and how it compliments who you have become.

"And God said unto Moses, I AM THAT I AM: and he said, Thus shalt thou say unto the children of Israel, I AM hath sent me unto you." (Exodus: 3:14 – KJV)

A LISTENING HEART

Dear Lord Jesus…

I come before you with a humbled heart. I would like to thank you for all the blessings you have given to me. Thank you for the first breath I breathe and have continued to breathe, to this day and beyond should you will it. Thank you Lord.

I may not know exactly how to approach you Lord, but I am willing to try. Teach me how to establish a personal relationship with you. Teach me how to share what is in my heart with you. Teach me how to speak to you; teach me how to spend time with you. Teach me Lord.

Help me understand how to talk to you and allow you to be a part of my life. Help me to listen for your voice, your guidance, your direction. Help me Lord.

Lead me Lord into your truth. Lead me into your righteousness. Lead me into your marvelous light. Lead me into your perfect love. Lead Me Lord.

Mold me into the person you imagined me to be when you formed me in my mother's womb. Mold me into your holiness. Mold me into the image of you. Mold Me Lord.

Please watch over my life Lord as I learn about you, and, develop my relationship with you. Please keep your hand over me in this life as well as in the hereafter. Watch over me Lord.

Thank you Lord for your gentle stirrings in my heart that made me aware, I need something more. Thank you for making me realize something was missing in my life. Thank you for showing me that it was you all along.

Thought for the day: Please accept my adoration Lord Jesus. Please accept my attempts to worship you. Please continue to wait patiently for me to learn how to allow you to teach me, help me, lead me and mold me, as I completely surrender myself to you.

"Lead me in thy truth, and teach me: for thou art the God of my salvation; on thee do I wait all the day."
(Psalms 25:5 - KJV)

SPEAK A BLESSING

"Sticks and stones may break your bones but names can never hurt you." Whoever coined that statement may want to rethink it. Words do hurt. Sometimes they cut deeper than an actual cut to the body. Words can make or break a person's career opportunities; they could be the difference between mending a relationship and tearing it apart. Words, as you speak them, can tell a lot about you, and your character.

Too often, we try to play down what someone says to us as unimportant, insignificant or even ineffective. If we could see our heart's scars and wounds, how many would you say where there from hateful, mean, vindictive and yes, even malicious words?

We should always think about our words before we speak them; as once spoken they can never be unspoken. We need to practice using our words for uplifting and inspiring purposes, not for tearing down and destroying.

Thought for the day: I challenge you to eliminate all negative words from being spoken by you today. When you speak,

speak a blessing and watch how they respond. I am positive you will realize just how powerful your words truly are.

"A word fitly spoken is like apples of gold in pictures of silver." (Proverbs 25:11 - KJV)

MAKE ME-OVER

Makeovers seem to be the new trend. Kitchen makeover, remodel your home, restoration of old cars, even personal makeovers of the body and the face. It appears that changing physically whether it is your personal appearance or enhancing your dwelling place, to a higher standard is coveted greatly.

We have a vision of what we think our home should look like, the type of car we drive and even ourselves. I think it would be safe to say that we are never truly satisfied with how others perceive our stature in life, and yes, even we ourselves are not satisfied with our own self-image.

The problem with physical makeovers, whether it is your home, your car, or your outer image, it eventually needs to be redone. It becomes old, cracked, out dated and, you find yourself doing it over again and again.

Here is a question, have you ever thought about giving your spirituality a makeover? Have you ever thought about what image God sees when He looks at you? Has your spirituality received a makeover since you became a believer?

When we become children of God, the Bible says that we old things pass away and we become as "new creatures." Have you experienced this makeover? Better yet, how will you know if you have received God's makeover? It is simple. We begin to take on the image of Christ. Do you see Christ in you when you look in the mirror?

God's makeover consists of growing in the fruit of the spirit as outlined in Galatians 5. Check it out and see if your spiritual makeover meets God's expectation. In truth, it is His makeover that will count in the end.

Thought for the day: Examine yourself to see if you portray the Fruit of the Spirit. If not, ask God to give you His makeover that will never grow old, dim, or go out of style. His makeover will last you a lifetime; and that is a makeover worth investing in!

"And God said, let us make man in our image, after our likeness..." (Genesis 1:26 - KJV)

FAITH THAT CONQUERS FEAR

Have you ever felt like God was calling you to do something, but you were afraid to take that initial step towards doing it? Let us look at Peter in the Bible, when Jesus bid him to come and walk on the water with Him.

Peter did not hesitate, in fact obeyed; and, acted on his faith by taking that initial step. With his eyes fixed on Jesus, Peter boldly stepped out of the boat and onto the water.

What I find so beautiful about this story, is that Peter was willing to put his faith into action. I can only imagine the adoration Jesus felt for Peter at that very moment. As the story goes, Peter allowed fear to well up inside of him, and soon felt as if he was sinking. With a cry, Peter called to Jesus, who quickly rescued him.

The Lord may be bidding you to leave your comfort zone, your safety net, your "boat" per se, and take the step Peter did; the step which activated his faith. If God calls you to do something, rest assured He will do everything in His power to secure your success. In other words, if necessary, you too can "walk on water."

Thought for the day: If you feel as though God is bidding you to do something for him, be a Peter, allow your faith to conquer fear.

"For God hath not given us the spirit of fear; but of power, and of love, and of a sound mind."
(2 Timothy 1:7 - KJV)

SEE WITH YOUR HEART NOT YOUR EYES

There is an old cliché` that says, "Looks can be deceiving."
When reflecting on this statement, I revert back to the religious
leaders that Jesus rebuked. When rebuking them, Jesus
basically told them that they "looked the part" but their hearts
were full of pride and they were far from the faithful followers
he was seeking and ultimately chose. Jesus picked twelve
ordinary men, and equipped them to do the extraordinary.
Could it be that Jesus' choice may have been the very reason
the religious leaders did not want to believe he was the long
awaited Messiah and sought to destroy him?

Surely the Messiah would not rebuke them; they were the
ones the people looked to, and perceived, as holy, skilled in the
reading and knowledge of the scriptures. How dare this Jesus,
a common carpenter come into their temple and tell them the
laws of God.

Too often we see people and value them based on how they
dress, level of education, color of their skin or gender, and yes,
even their beliefs. If they do not look the part or speak with
elegance, we often discard them as useless or insignificant.

Jesus taught us a valuable lesson … looks definitely can be deceiving. When looking at those around you, look with your heart, not your eyes.

Thought for the day: Take a moment, and think about what people would see; if they looked with their heart and not their eyes at you.

"This people draweth nigh unto me with their mouth, and honoureth me with their lips; but their heart is far from me." (Matthew 15:8 - KJV)

NO WORRIES

Sometimes we make life more difficult that it really is. If we would only allow ourselves to not only listen to the voice of God, but obey His will for our lives, we could eliminate so much heartache from touching our lives. Why are we so stubborn? We pray about our situation, we say we are listening for God's direction but do we really seek his direction or are we just praying to pray?

Often our family and friends will give us good, solid, and sound advice but instead of taking it, we ultimately do it our way.

The Bible teaches us that God has our best interest at heart and he doesn't want us to worry, fret, and be fearful or weary. Yet we continue to live lives that are less that desirable, full of stress, hurt, pain, obstacles and far beneath the blessings that are ours for the taking. We become overwhelmed with life and wonder if we will ever see light at the end of the tunnel.

If you are tired of living a sub-standard life, and want something better, you have to try something that you have not tried before. There is a saying "if you keep doing the same thing the same way you will always get the same result. You have done it your way, and, how is that working for you? Perhaps it is time to switch it up and try God's way. What do you have to lose… pain, sorrow, worry, burdens, etc., I say, go for it.

Thought for the day: Think about what is going wrong in your life today; then go to Him in prayer and ask him to help you surrender it unto His will for your life.

"Take my yoke upon you, and learn of me; for I am meek and lowly in heart: and ye shall find rest unto your souls." (Matthew 11:29 - KJV)

FROZEN IN TIME

We may not always understand why God does the things he does, but one thing for sure we must understand is when God tells us to do something, we better think twice about disobeying him. At least that stands true for Lot's wife.

Thinking about the direct orders God gave Lot and his family. God told Lot to get his family out of the City of Sodom as he was going to destroy it and its sister city Gomorrah. In addition, He told them to *flee the city and not to look back.*

In her disobedience of God's direct order, Lot's wife was turned into a pillar of salt when she looked back at the City of Sodom. I have often wondered why God did that. What was the purpose, what did he want us to learn from this drastic event.

Could it be that God turned her into that pillar because she couldn't or perhaps wouldn't let go of what God wanted her to let go of? Perhaps God perceived she wanted the evil city more than she wanted Him. With that disobedient act, she became a statute, a landmark, or a monument if you will. She became a reminder for all that gazed upon it. She became frozen in time, stuck in a position of looking backwards instead of forward; and I would venture to say portraying a look of regret on her face.

It would be safe to surmise God was teaching us a grave lesson…obey Him! Let go of the things that hold us down, or keep us in a state of stagnation; and to look forward, and to never turn back. Oftentimes we are so afraid of change that we hold onto things that God may be trying to get us to turn loose; and because we refuse to we miss our blessings.

Thought for the day: Has God been talking to you? Has he instructed you to let go of something but you are still holding onto it? Have you become your own monument, frozen in time? If so, break free today...and never look back!

"My sheep hear my voice, and I know them, and they follow me."
(John 10:27-KJV)

THE KINGDOM AWAITS

Have you ever said to yourself "Life is just not fair?" I do my best everyday but it just does not seem to be good enough.

You see other folks being blessed abundantly and wonder, why them Lord, and why not me? What are they doing so right to get this or that? I serve you Lord with all my heart, all my might, but my life is just not what I thought it would be, or should be. You ask, "When Lord, when will it be my turn?"

Believe it or not, this is exactly what the enemy would have us think. When we start to murmur and allow our hearts to get entangled in jealousies, strife's and coveting things as our main focus, it leaves little room for being grateful for what God has blessed us with.

Stop this very moment and give thanks to God for your blessings. No matter how small or big it is, give thanks for it.

There is one thing that the enemy wants us to forget, our promise! We have a hope. We have a promise as God's children… the promise of life beyond our imagination; more than we could ever imagine; heaven will be our home and everything in it!

So don't let yourself be caught up on temporal happiness. It's true that this life may not be fair, but our eternal life will be, as it is promised. We WILL have our happily ever after.

Thought for the day: Remind yourself throughout the day that no matter what happens, in the end you WIN. Not only will you partake in every blessing in Heaven, but you will rein with your Savior. And what a reward it will be.

"But as it is written, Eye hath not seen, nor ear heard, neither have entered into the heart of man, the things which God hath prepared for them that love him."
(1 Corinthians 2:9 -KJV)

TELL YOUR STORY

Too often we hear people talking about their religion. I was taught this, or that. When you get down to the nuts and bolts of the religious realm, we have to understand that it is not about religion but an actual relationship with God that we need to be concerned with. Doctrinal differences when argued in heated debates with others can destroy a person who is searching for God.

Do not go there. Plain and simple, do not argue with someone over what you believe. Instead talk about true events. Talk about what God has done for you personally. Talk about your love from Christ. That is where you will peak their interest.

It is through your personal experience that you share with others which will encourage them to want to seek out their own personal relationship with God. It is about how often they hear you speak about the God that created you. How often do you talk to others about what God has done for you, personally?

Share how God has healed your body, or met a financial need that seemed impossible, or how he has become your own personal friend. These are the things that will open the door to successful witnessing; your own report of what God has done for you!

If there is someone you want God do something special in their life, share your testimony with them and watch what God does. Share how Jesus was sent to us for us!

Thought for the day: I challenge you to talk about your own personal relationship with God with others instead of the scriptures; you will see a hungry heart for more. It is this report that will win their hearts to Christ.

"And we have seen and do testify that the Father sent the Son to be the Saviour of the world."
(1John 4:14 – KJV)

SHARING WORDS OF LOVE

I need you; I love you. I adore you. I cherish you. These are a few phrases which make us feel good when we hear them, especially when it is said by someone special to us. By someone we feel the same towards, someone we love. These expressions of endearments make us smile, uplift us, encourages us, sustains us. When we hear them, we feel needed. We feel loved.

It is always nice to know you are loved and being thought of. It makes us feel warm and fuzzy inside. You know how you feel when you receive these words, but when was the last time you told someone these things? More importantly, when was the last time you told God that you need Him, love Him, adore Him and cherish Him. When was the last time you spent time with Him? Just like you, He enjoys hearing how you feel about Him. After all, He did create you.

Thought for the day: If you have not already done it, why not take a moment to tell God just how much you love Him. Think of one thing that God has done for you and take time to say thank you.

"For God so loved the world, that he gave his only begotten Son, that whosoever believeth in him should not perish, but have everlasting life." (John 3:16 - KJV)

FIRST IMPRESSIONS

Have you ever been in the grocery store and saw a mother yank up their child by the arm screaming at him or her to stop it and be quiet? Or have you experienced the impatience of a driver behind you that suddenly speeds ahead of you, and you know they have spewed out a beret of expletive's to you? At that very moment, you form an opinion, an impression if you will, of that person even though you know nothing about them. We all do it without even thinking about it.

The unfortunate part of first impressions is that they are not always true of who that person is. That mother may have been up for hours dealing with a sick husband, trying to budget the household finances, or she, herself may be sick, worn down and had reached her breaking point. That enraged driver may have been warned if they are late for work one more time they will be fired; or rushing to the hospital to be with a dying loved one.

Circumstances cause us to react differently than we normally would under different circumstances. Forming first impressions can be damaging and so far from the truth of whom that person really is. In fact, more often than not, we tend to form an impression that is negative rather than positive.

Often we fail to realize that how we interact with others leaves an impression with them. Depending on what you show that person will depend on the type of impression you leave them with. Remember everyone has bad days. We need to take that into account before we form the opinion that someone is a terrible mother, or labeled another as a "road rage maniac".

It is important to think before reacting to a situation because once you have reacted to that situation that becomes their impression of you.

Perhaps this is the reason God teaches us not to judge as we have no idea what that person may be facing, battling or struggling with.

Learn to be an encourager. When someone is showing their less than desirable side of themself, don't form an impression, but instead say a prayer for them, or better yet if possible, ask if you can be a help to them. Let them see the love of Christ in you instead of the judgment of the world.

In doing this, their first impression of you, will be good, and perhaps will last a lifetime.

Thought for the day: If the opportunity arises today wherein you can change someone's first impression of you, take the opportunity and run with it.

"Let not then your good be evil spoken of."
(Romans 14:16 - KJV)

CHIRST-LIKE

Too often I find myself in a position when I look back on a situation I think, "I should have handled that better", or "WOW I really missed an opportunity to allow Christ to shine through me". How could I have fallen into that trap, I know better. Have you ever been there?

Do not beat yourself up over it. We all have those less then desirable moments. The good news is we are able to recognize our shortcomings, missteps as you will, and have the ability to learn from our mistakes. Do not dwell on them. When you ask God for forgiveness of the wrongdoing, he forgets about it; so you should too!

Instead, we must ask God to give us hearts that obey without questioning motives, and faith that is unwavering under any situation. We need to pursue being an encourager with our words, thoughts, and deeds, but even more so, we need to ask God to instill in us, His love, His wisdom, His forgiveness, His character, His kindnesses, etc.

When we possess these traits, then we can say, "I've done my best" and God expects nothing more than that.

Thought for the day: Start today, start fresh. Remember that you are unable to change the past, so leave the past in the past and embrace who you are today.

"It is of the LORD'S mercies that we are not consumed, because his compassions fail not."
(Lam 3:22 – KJV)

ROLE MODEL

Have you ever really thought about how much influence you have in other people's lives? As a parent, or an older brother or sister, you help shape your children or brothers and or sisters. How you act or even react to situations leaves an impression.

The words you choose, whether they are uplifting or degrading can make someone's day or break it. The places you go or even choose to take your children or siblings can form morals or destroy them. Everything we do has some form of impact on our own lives and the lives around us. In truth, we influence others whether we realize it or not, and that influence is either good or bad.

Just think, you can either help someone find Jesus or you can help lead them away from Him. If you tell people you are a Christian, do your actions validate those words? Or better yet, do your actions validate you are a Christian?

How you act, what you say and where you go can do one of two things... lead someone to God... or lead them away from God. Which do you do?

Thought for the day: Whether you realize it or not, there is someone watching your life. It could be a co-worker, your neighbor, someone in your congregation, or perhaps someone even closer to you; your spouse, your children. What is your life saying to them? Take time out today and think about what kind of example you are showing those around you. If you feel you are setting the wrong example, make a concerted effort to start setting an example that is not only pleasing to you, but pleasing to God. Become the role model YOU would look up to.

"For I have given you an example, that ye should do as I have done to you." (John: 13:15 – KJV)

WHAT'S IN YOUR ALABASTER BOX?

We have all heard the story of the woman with her Alabaster Box. We know how she took the box, broke it open and poured the precious oils over the head of Jesus. We also know how she cried and with her tears she washed the feet of the Master and then dried them with her hair.

Alabaster was very expensive in biblical times. Additionally, alabaster was used for important purposes only. So you can just imagine the disbelief as well as anger of the Pharisees when they saw this less than desirable woman not only possessed the expensive Alabaster box, but that she broke it open and wasted the precious oil. Unfortunately for those in attendance, they could not see nor understand what she was presenting to Jesus. But Jesus did.

This woman, who is believed to have been Mary, had very little, was scorned amongst the people as a sinner or worse, a prostitute. She knew the importance of who Jesus was. She wanted to show her appreciation to Him. She took what was possibly her most prized possession and selflessly used it as an act of love, adoration and honor to Jesus.

35

Just picture the scene, a scorned woman, crying at the feet of Jesus; and Jesus allowing her to wash his feet with her hair. Haven't we been there ourselves as scorned sinners crying before the Master? However, Jesus has asked nothing of us but to love Him and follow His ways.

But what if! What if Jesus required a prized possession from each of us? What would you offer up to Him? Would you offer up to Him your prized possession, or would you give something that holds less value to you because the other was just too precious to part with?

If you wanted to show your love, adoration and honor to Jesus, just as this woman did, what would be in your Alabaster Box?

Thought for the day: Unfortunately it seems that we may put too much emphasis on our possessions than the One who blessed us with those possessions. However, the moral of the story was not what she offered; it was her willingness to sacrifice the sacred possession to Jesus and asking nothing in return. If you have forgotten to simply love Jesus because of who He is, I urge you today to re-read the story of the Alabaster Box. And then ask yourself, have you had an Alabaster Box experience before Jesus and is your relationship with Him a memorial of you?

"Verily I say unto you, Wheresoever this gospel shall be preached throughout the whole world, this also that she hath done shall be spoken of for a memorial of her."
(Mark 14:9 – KJV)

HERE WE GO AGAIN...

Have you ever had a "ground hog experience?" You know that thing that keeps happening over and over again in your life and you just can't seem to get past it? I think we all have had this experience; and we question, "Why does this keep happening to me?" or find you saying "Here we go again..." In honesty, I believe God allows it to happen. In fact, it appears to be a test.

We do not face our temptations or weaknesses once in our lifetime, no, unfortunately we face them multiple times. We need to overcome the things that upset us. We need to be watchful and see how we react to the same circumstances in our lives. If we continue to do the same thing over and over again and expect a different outcome, well, we are only fooling ourselves as it won't happen.

God knows our weakness, our areas of temptations and he will allow us to continue to go through the struggle until we are victorious over the enemy's hold on that area of our lives. We need to look to Him to help us become overcomers.

Once we have mastered these areas of our lives we do not seem to go through that particular circumstance again or find ourselves saying "Here we go again." Instead, we will see what God was doing all along in us... we will see growth.

Thought for the day: If you find that you are struggling with the same situation over and over again in your life, I urge you to take time throughout the day to plan out a new approach to the problem. Look at it from a fresh perspective and ask God to help you to yield to the change he is trying to make in you.

"Therefore if any man be in Christ, he is a new creature: old things are passed away; behold, all things are become new."
(2 Corinthians 5:17 – KJV)

SPIRITUAL EYES

When you look at God's creation you see the beauty for the most part. You are not looking at the trees, the mountains, and the ocean with a critical eye. If you are anything like me, you are looking through the eyes of wonderment. We look through the eyes of how beautiful, how awesome, how spacious, and how amazing.

What if we looked at each other in the same wonderment? What if when we looked at our fellow man we saw their uniqueness instead of seeing their flaws? I propose that we all see each other through spiritual eyes as opposed to human eyes. You may ask what the difference is. What is the difference between human eyes and spiritual eyes? Human eyes you see their flaws, spiritual eyes you see their potential.

Thought for the day: Should you see someone and begin to look at them critically, stop yourself and try to see them through spiritual eyes instead of human eyes. Then assess the difference in how you truly see that person.

"But blessed are your eyes, for they see: and your ears, for they hear." (Mat 13:16 –KJV)

WE ARE WONDERFULLY MADE

Have you ever just wondered how many thoughts, words, expressions have gone through your mind on a twenty-four hour period; or just an hour. I would venture to say that we could not count them nor remember every word that crossed our mind. Ah, but God does. He remembers every word, every expression, everything about us.

It is truly amazing how the Creator created us to be simple beings, but with such complexities as well.

Think about all the bones, vessels, blood and mass that our bodies are made of. If that does not make you shake your head in wonderment, I don't know what would.

What about our outer structure. Our eyes, our ears, mouth, nose, hair, you get the picture. To know that the God of the universe loved me so much that he took such care when he created me is beyond comprehension. He created only one of me. I am unique. I am an original. I am one of a kind.

To believe that we just "evolved" is incomprehensible. To think that we just "happened" takes the beauty out of our separation from all other creatures. I do not know about you, but I choose to believe that a Higher Power took the time to ponder my existence, envisions who I would be and then, personally created me.

Thought for the day: Take some time to think about all the intricate parts of your being and then give thanks to God for being such a loving, caring, and personalized Creator.

"I will praise thee; for I am fearfully and wonderfully made: marvellous are thy works; and that my soul knoweth right well."
(Psalms 139:14 – KJV)

VALLEY OF INDECISION

I have been thinking a lot about choice. Sometimes there are too many choices and therefore it's easier not to make the decision. Or perhaps we are afraid to make a choice because we are fearful we will make the wrong one. We contemplate all the "what if's" only to find ourselves at the end of the day still not closer to making the choice. You find yourself in the valley of indecision, stagnation, a place of no movement.

Well, unfortunately, I have found that while we are in the land of indecision, choices are being made all around us that may, or may not, affect us. I think I would rather make a choice whether it is right or wrong, than have someone else make it for me. At least this way, if it turns out right I do not have someone saying "aren't you glad I made that decision for you" or worse yet those dreaded words "I told you so".

I believe that God sometimes remains silent merely because he is waiting for us to take that leap of faith and make a choice so he can perfect the outcome accordingly. Face it, you will never know until you try so why not take a deep breath, and jump.

Thought for the day: If there is a decision that you have been prolonging in making, stop procrastinating, weigh your pros and cons, overcome your fear, pray and ask God to bless your choice and make it.

"The LORD is on my side; I will not fear: what can man do unto me?" (Psalms 118:6 – KJV)

THROUGH THE STORM

We all go through storms. If we did not, we would not grow. Storms in life whether we want to admit it or not, shape us into whom we become. They can show us how strong we are, or how weak. They can push us to try harder, or give up. They can encourage us, or defeat us. But the ultimate outcome of the storm depends on us.

If we could just get a handle on what these storms truly are in our lives we can embrace them instead of run from them. We can look to them as the challenges they are, and divide and conquer it before it conquers us.

As with any storm, it gets darkest during the heart of the storm, but soon, it begins to let up, and the light begins to peak through and the storm subsides, and soon dissipates. It is the same with our personal storms. God is with you. Do not give up; your breakthrough could be just around the corner. You have weathered the worst of it; your victory could be a minute, an hour or a day away. At any rate, your deliverance is closer today than it was yesterday, and, tomorrow just may be the breakthrough you have been waiting for.

Often the enemy will tell us to throw in the towel. The battle is too hard. We cannot win. God does not care. He has forsaken you. You are all alone. **DO NOT BELIEVE HIS LIES!** Remember, the enemy only fights you the hardest when he knows you are headed for a blessing for your steadfast faithfulness. Do not allow him to rob you of your blessing!

Thought for the day: If you are in a storm, I encourage you - do not give up! Keep pressing through, today just may be your day of salvation.

"Ye shall not need to fight in this battle: set yourselves, stand ye still, and see the salvation of the LORD with you, O Judah and Jerusalem: fear not, nor be dismayed; to morrow go out against them: for the LORD will be with you."
(2Ch.20:17- KJV)

NO GIANT IS TOO TALL

We all have heard of underdogs. In fact, you may have been considered an underdog at some point in your life. Or perhaps you were seen as a misfit. Someone that just did not belong, or needed protection. Someone that would not, or could not, hurt a fly. David, the youngest son of Jesse perhaps was seen as such a boy.

The Bible teaches us that David was summoned by his father to go down to the war camp to check on the welfare of his brothers. As he entered the camp he heard all the chatter about some giant. While in the camp however, David heard and seen the mighty warrior Goliath shouting his daily threats and David's curiosity got the best of him. David asked of his brothers, "Who is this uncircumcised Philistine that he should defy the armies of God?"

David saw that the men of valor were afraid of the Philistine. However, David being fearless said he would fight against the giant. The story goes on to say that even his own brothers scorned him saying that he was just a boy and stood no chance of winning a challenge against the giant. King Saul was just as skeptical. Nonetheless with David's persistence, King Saul consented to allow David to challenge Goliath.

They attempted to garb him in armor and sword, but because of the weight of the armor David buckled under it. He shed the armor and sword and adorned himself in his shepherd's clothes, his staff, sling and five stones to approach Goliath. Goliath laughed at David. He could not believe this little boy was there to defy him, to destroy him, much less kill him.

"Then said David to the Philistine, Thou comest to me with a sword, and with a spear, and with a shield: but I come to thee in the name of the LORD of hosts, the God of the armies of Israel, whom thou hast defied." (I Sam. 17-45 – KJV)

We know how the story ends, David kills Goliath, and he later becomes King.

David was the underdog for sure; however he had the power of the Almighty God on his side. David knew that in his own strength he could not defeat the enemy, but by putting his complete trust and faith in his God, he believed he would be victorious and win the battle.

Thought for the day: Facing a Giant in your own life? Is there someone or something you are battling in your own life that seems insurmountable? Perhaps God is waiting for you to have faith like David, to rely on Him to fight the battle for you and claim the victory even before it happens. Why not declare the power of the Almighty God over the situation and watch God make your impossible battle possible.

"I can do all things through Christ which strengtheneth me."
(Phl. 4:13 – KJV)

I CHOOSE

I choose to be happy today. I will not allow the pressures of the day defeat me. I will not let the stresses of baskets full of laundry, dirty dishes, crying babies to get me down today. I will not allow any negative thoughts to enter my mind. I will not view the glass as being half empty, but will see it as half full.

I choose to see the positive in everything that happens to me today regardless of the negative connotations that may be underlying the situation.

I choose to smile at adversity today. I choose to smile from the inside out; and laugh in the face of that adversity.

I choose to be an encourager today. I choose to say something uplifting to you even if you do not want to hear it.

I choose to be a blessing to everyone that crosses my path this day.

I choose to say thank you God for allowing me to awake to a new day.

I choose to see God's beautiful fingerprint in his creation today, instead of the ugliness of the world.

I choose to exercise the "pay it forward" gesture today in honor of God's commandment to "love one another."

I choose to put a song on my lips.

I choose to love; not hate.

I choose to live my faith. *I choose!*

Thought for the day: I choose; two very powerful words. You are in control of the choices you make. You can either seize the day, or let the day seize you. The choice is yours. So I ask you, what will you choose today?

"A merry heart doeth good like a medicine:
but a broken spirit drieth the bones."
(Pro. 17:22 – KJV)

DO YOU BELIEVE?

If you are truly a believer in Christ, then you believe the words in the Bible are true. You believe that God gave His son Jesus and He is your Savior. You believe God can do anything. You believe that God watches over you. You believe that God loves you unconditionally. You believe.

So why do you worry? Why do you allow the enemy to get you so tangled up in fear, worry, doubt and disbelief? Why do you fret about the unpaid bills on your table? Or the husband that just lost his job? The doctors say the reports do not look good. Why do you allow your circumstances dictate your level of believe, or worse, unbelief?

Stop giving the enemy power. He only has power in your life because you give it to him. Take back the power and realize that you hold the answer to all your woes, with one word. Faith.

If you need deliverance from something, just believe you have that deliverance! Speak your miracle into reality. Activate your faith by truly believing that your God can and will do the impossible for you. Do not allow doubt, fear, worry or even indecisiveness to rob you of what is rightfully yours… deliverance, victory!

Thought for the day: As a believer you are entitled to the promises in the Bible. So I encourage you to test God. That's right, you heard me. Test God to do what he has promised in His Word. If you believe with as little as a mustard seed, God will deliver! So what are you waiting for, move that mountain.

"And Jesus said unto them, Because of your unbelief: for verily I say unto you, If ye have faith as a grain of mustard seed, ye shall say unto this mountain, Remove hence to yonder place; and it shall remove; and nothing shall be impossible unto you. "(Mat. 17:20 – KJV)

I HEAR VOICES

Have you ever found yourself in the land of decision and suddenly everyone is giving you their opinion and or advice on what you should do. One person may be telling you to stay, while another is telling you to go. Perhaps another is telling you that you need to just wait a little while longer. However, all along, you are hearing an entirely different answer within yourself.

I call this situation, hearing voices. The voices around you are so loud sometimes that you can hardly hear yourself think; much less make a decisions.

Too often we listen to the wrong voice. In listening to the wrong voice, we perhaps travel a journey that was not ours to travel. In fact, listening to the wrong voice may take you so far off the path of what God intended for you, it may take years to re-group.

An exercise I have found to be quite helpful in these situations is to pray. Pray and ask God to give you clarity on what He wants you to do; and then wait. Waiting of course is the hardest part of this journey, but essential. While in the waiting process, take the time to review your situation, align it with the Word of God, ask the hard questions, would this take me closer to God or take me further away from Him. During this assessment, continue to pray, and listen. Listen for the one true voice that will never steer you in the wrong direction.

How will you know when you have heard that voice? You will no longer feel confused, torn, or conflicted. You will have peace, blessed assurance and confidence that the decision you made is the right one.

Sometimes hearing voices can be a good thing because it prepares you to listen for the right voice.

Thought for the day: If you are in the middle of making a major decision in your life, do not make that decision in haste. Also, do not allow your decision-making to be based on what others view as the answer, take it to the Lord in prayer, ask him for clarity and be patient enough to wait. Wait until you hear the one voice that matters.

"Wait on the LORD: be of good courage, and he shall strengthen thine heart: wait, I say, on the LORD."
(Psalms 27:14 – KJV)

FREE INDEED

What is the most liberating feeling in the world? A heart free of hurt, rebellion, strife, hatred, or revenge is one of God's greatest gifts. When you can awake to a new day and not feel the sting of yesterday's hurts you have truly received a loving heart.

I think about all the awful things that Jesus went through. They scorned Him, they mocked Him, they beat Him, made fun of Him, and yet He loved them. All the way to the cross He maintained His humbled giving heart. Talk about a forgiving heart!

Too often we get hurt and we are unable, or should I say unwilling to let the hurt go. We feel like they owe us an apology and even when we get one, we still feel wounded. Some even go as far as wanting revenge. Get even. Or worse, plot to hurt them back.

When we do not let go of the wound and we continue to pick at it, it just festers into a sore than stays open, raw, pus-filled and unable to mend.

However, if we clean it, wash it and nurse the wound, eventually it begins to scab over and soon it has healed. Some wounds will leave a scar, while others just disappear.

Forgiveness works a lot like this process. When we hold on to the hurt, we allow ourselves to become bitter, resentful, hateful and all that leads to bondage. We are bound up with these emotions and unfortunately turn our once happy life into an unhappy one.

Do not allow yourself to get caught up in this web. Learn to let the bad go, put it in capable hands of Jesus to handle and let it go. When you can free your heart of these feelings, it is left the way God intended it, filled with love and acceptance.

Thought for the day: If you are harboring feelings that are keeping you bound up in unhappy thoughts and emotions, take time today to assess why you haven't let go of the hurt. Is the hurt worth your peace, joy and contentment in your life? I would think not. Instead of continuing in these feelings, take it to the Master in prayer and ask Him to not only give you a heart of forgiveness over it; but pray for the person who caused you such grief. Allow yourself to become free, free indeed.

"Then came Peter to him, and said, Lord, how oft shall my brother sin against me, and I forgive him? Till seven times? Jesus saith unto him, I say not unto tee, Until seven times: but, Until seventy times seven." (Matthew 18:21-22 KJV)

HIDE ME O LORD

There is a famous line from the movie **"Forrest Gump"** wherein Jenny yells to her friend, "run Forrest, run", all the while she is trying to deter the pursuers. In this case they were the enemy, the bullies. She wanted to protect her friend. She put herself in harm's way in order to help her friend reach safety.

We may find ourselves at the wrong place at the wrong time, yet instead of fleeing we remain in the midst of the turmoil. You may have a nagging feeling in your gut that you need to run, but you do not act on it. Even before you are able to realize what is happening, you may be caught up in the wrongdoing and suddenly wishing you were anywhere but there.

That nagging feeling in your gut, often known as intuition should never be ignored. Not only is it a built in warning bell, but it is your inner voice of reason. Some even call it the voice of *God.*

When you are in situations and the hair on the back of your neck rises up, you need to take notice. Or if you begin to feel uneasy, insecure or even frightened, this is your queue to run!

Believe it or not, those feelings are the voice of Forrest's friend Jenny. Better yet know as your own personal God. It is your internal protector telling you that something is not quite right and you should run as fast as you can. Run.

The enemy will try to lead you into temptation. Lead you into sin. Lead you down the road of self-destruction if possible. If you do not listen to your inner-voice, the pathway may appear appealing, enticing or even thrilling and you will follow. Once the enemy has you in his grip, all the glitz and glitter becomes dull, tarnished and unfulfilling. You find yourself wondering how in the world you get out of the mess you have found yourself in.

There is hope. You can be rescued. God is always with you. He is aware of your surroundings, and what is lurking around the corner to trip you up; or harm you. However, there is one thing that God does for you that Jenny was unable to do for her friend. God can always make a way of escape. Do not stay in the midst of the turmoil, tune in to your inner voice and get your plan of escape!

Thought for the day: Have you traveled down the wrong pathway and are feeling lost, trapped or hopeless? Do not despair, God is fully aware and is able to help. Go to Him in prayer today, ask him to rescue you and look for the open door. He will provide it.

"Deliver me O LORD, from mine enemies. I flee unto thee to hide me." (Psalms 143:9 – KJV)

TOUCH SOMEONE

In this day and age of technology, it is so easy to remove the personal touch from our communications. Through email, text notifications, even voicemail, we no longer have to physically reach out to touch someone.

I have found that although all this technology may be good in business, it may not be the best for one's personal life. When reading an email or a text we lose the ability to read body language, or see the expression on their face as they speak. We have no true way of knowing if the words we are reading are true or fiction, surface or heartfelt.

Perhaps we need to slow things down a bit and put a little "old fashion" back into our day. Maybe sit down and write out a greeting card, or pen a love letter; or make a batch of cookies for that loved one you have been thinking about and drive them over to them instead of giving them an online virtual dessert. It may be exactly what the doctor ordered. Nothing beats a face to face connection.

Thought for the day: Perhaps you are feeling like you have lost a personal connection with someone important to you, why not make plans to reach out to them today, and spend some one-on-one time together. Make it personal.

"A man that hath friends must shew himself friendly:
and there is a friend that sticketh closer than a brother."
(Proverbs 18:24 – KJV)

WHOSE MIND IS IT ANYWAY

The mind is a very unique and puzzling thing. If life turned out exactly how we picture it in our minds, we would never face adversity, ever learn how to overcome challenges, exercise faith or pursue our dreams. Life would be perfect without any effort. I think life would be unrewarding and without inspiration if we were given everything exactly how we dreamed it. When things do not turn out the way we see it that is where the real struggle begins.

In truth it is our thoughts about how something should turn out, or be in our lives that get us in trouble. We have this preconceived notion of how something should be; and when it does not turn out that way, we are devastated. We have to learn that although we can visualize something does not mean that is truly how it should be or will be. Too often we put all our energy into making our fantasy our reality when in fact God has placed the obstacles in the way for a reason.

We have to stop thinking about how we perceive something should be and just let it happen...ultimately it's going to turn out how God designed it; not how you pictured it to be.

Thought for the day: Do not allow yourself to get caught up in your thoughts of how a situation in your life should turn out. Trust God and watch have your story unfolds.

"For who hath known the mind of the Lord, that he may instruct him? But we have the mind of Christ."
(I Co.2:16 – KJV)

YOUR CRIES NEVER FALL ON A DEAF EAR

The Bible is full of stories about crying out to the Lord for help. One that sticks out is the cry of Jehoshaphat. He not only was the king of Judah but he was a mighty warrior too. He was used to facing adversity. So you can imagine his surprise when he entered into this particular battle he found himself in trouble. Through no fault of his own but a mistaken identity claim by the chariot commanders, the story tells how Jehoshaphat was heavily pursued by the enemy. The beauty of the story is that Jehoshaphat did not let that stop or deter his determination to win the battle.

Instead of feeling defeated or surrendering he did the only thing he knew to do, he cried out to God to help him; and guess what? God did. God heard his cry! Through God's infinite wisdom and power, He drew the enemy away from the one who cried out for His help. Had Jehoshaphat not cried out, it is quite probable that he would have been overtaken by the group and lost his life right there on that battlefield.

Let us remember as we face our own battles today, our true strength and protection does not come from within us, but it comes from God. We should never wait until we are beaten down, weak, defeated or without hope before we begin to ask God for help. When the enemy attacks, or at the first sign of trouble, we should follow Jehoshaphat's lead. We should never hesitate to cry out… "God I need you, please help me". However, it does not stop there, we must believe that God will hear our cry, and then stand still and see the salvation of the Lord come to our rescue.

Thought for the day: Is your enemy pursuing you and gaining ground? If so, stop what you are doing right now and cry out to God for His help. He is just a whisper away.

"What shall we then say to these things?
If God be for us, who can be against us?"
(Romans 8:31 – KJV)

WINDOWS TO THE SOUL

Do you remember the first time your heart was broken? Do you remember how you cried, and felt like you were going to die? How you swore you would never fall in love again and that you could never love anyone else the way you loved so and so?

Looking back we see the adolescence innocence through that thought process and even the pain. However, over time that adolescence innocence becomes a grown up hardened calloused, unyielding emotion. Life sure does have a way of hardening us up, does it not?

Too often we find ourselves broken hearted and nursing our wounds. A broken heart is hard to mend; and many times we do not mend it, we only mask it with walls we erect around it. We believe that if we shut that part of ourselves off we are protecting ourselves from feeling that way ever again. How wrong we are.

God never intended for us to function in part. He created the entire body to work in conjunction with all the other parts. When we close off a part of us, we are not fully functional;

therefore not complete. God created the human body to heal its wounds so it could become complete again.

As with any wound, it is first open to the pain. Secondly we have to push through the pain and clean it up to get a closer look at what truly happened. Then, we either wrap it up to protect it from the air and or germs that may get in it; or we consult a professional for a more serious wound. Lastly, and in due time, we unwrap the wound, to either find it healing nicely, or completely healed.

The operative phrase here is "in due time." Surface wounds and even emotional wounds take time to heal. We can speed up the process of healing by doing what the doctor orders or we can slow it down. The end results depend on us and how we allow or do not allow the process to proceed. So will you allow yourself to mend your broken spirit through God's perfect design of the human body and nature, or will you hold on to the hurt and keep the wound exposed indefinitely?

Thought for the day: If you have allowed yourself to erect walls to protect yourself from unwanted feelings, why not allow God to mead your broken spirit today. It is time to become whole again and experience a completely functional you. Just allow God to tear down those walls and replace them with the windows that were supposed to be there.

**"He healeth the broken in heart, and bindeth
up their wounds." (Psalms 147:3 – KJV)**

LET YOUR TESTIMONY SPEAK FOR YOU

Have you ever wondered why Testimonies are so important? In a court room it may be the difference between life and death; or in an accident the eye witness' testimony could determine who was at fault. But I'm talking about a different type of testimony today. I'm talking about YOUR personal testimony. Your trials, your experiences, your heartbreaks, your sufferings which at the time felt like they were unbearable, you would surely die. Yet through the grace of God he brings you through each and every one of them. Why does He do that? It's really simply; He wants us to share our testimony with others because it helps to encourage them. Perhaps they are going through a similar trial, test or heartache. It lets them know that they can continue to stand when the times get rough.

Have you ever looked at the word Testimony? The word itself defines its definition. If we take the first four letters of the word, what does it spell? Test. If we do not go through a test, we would have no testimony. Without a testimony, we cannot truly witness to others about the goodness, graciousness, power, faithfulness, and unconditional love of Chris. The beauty of a testimony is that you are not in it alone but God is with you during the "test" period and eventually turns it into an awesome testimony to be shared to encourage and grow our faith. Now that is a testimony worth sharing.

Thought for the day: If you are going through something, try to look at it from a fresh perspective. Look and find what the "test" is, and journalize your journey. At the end of the test, look back over your entries. Do you see the testimony God was forming in you? Now, go share it with the world.

"And he said unto them, Go ye into all the world, and preach the gospel to every creature."
(Mark 16:15 – KJV)

YOU TALKIN ` TO ME...

So often when we think about God calling someone to
do a work for him why do we look to others rather than to
ourselves? We immediately start to rationalize why God
could not possibly be calling us. We tell ourselves we are not
qualified, not intelligent enough, or worse yet, start to list all of
our flaws and weaknesses.

We can even identify ourselves with such a person as
Gideon in the Bible. Was not Gideon the least in his family
which in fact actually represented the weakest clan? However,
God chose him! God chose Gideon who was not the strongest,
the smartest, or even the most qualified for the job to lead
a small group of men (I believe less than 300) to defeat a
Midianite army that grossly outnumbered Gideon and his tiny
army of men.

It would be safe to say that Gideon was scared, I know if
we were in his boots I would be shaking in them! Gideon was
probably feeling hopeless knowing he was outnumbered in
men and wondering how God could put him in such a position.
Gideon knew other than having God on his side; he had

nothing going for him. Ah, but truth be known having just God he had exactly all he needed.

As the story unfolds, Gideon conquers and receives the victory; and through that victory peace was restored to the land for forty years.

God enjoys showing His power is strong in the weak and humble. Moses was the meekest man on earth; and David was well described as "ruddy". With the hand and the direction of the Lord over these men, victory was delivered into their hands and they have gone down in the history books not as they were first perceived but last perceived.

Thought for the day: Perhaps you are the least of your family, or feel you are the weakest. However, if you will allow it, God can take you from ordinary and make you extraordinary, and if you follow His lead, nothing or no one can hold you back. God is enough. He is calling you… so will you answer him or ignore him?

"Ye shall not need to fight in this battle: set yourselves, stand ye still, and see the salvation of the LORD with you, O Judah and Jerusalem: fear not, nor be dismayed; to morrow go out against them: for the LORD will be with you."
(2Ch 20:17 – KJV)

SWEET GIFT OF GOD

One of the sweetest gifts God gave us is the gift of the Holy Ghost. Through the Holy Ghost we have his spirit living within us. It is this spirit that strengthens us as one of His children. Through the Holy Ghost, and our obedience to it we learn to be overcomers. The Spirit gives us strength to endure life's circumstances, no matter what that may be. The Holy Ghost comforts us when we are sad, depressed, hurt, or lonely. It guides us throughout the obstacles that may be placed in our way, by opening our path during the journey.

The Holy Ghost also instructs us through the reading of His Word. With the reading of His Word it teaches us the difference between rights, wrongs, righteousness and unrighteousness, holiness, even avoiding temptations.

A final piece the Holy Ghost does that we rarely speak about is it convicts us. In other words, God's Spirit is at work in us, transforming us into a better person, into the image of Christ. The God of the universe loves us so much that instead of leaving us to our vises, he dwells within us. How blessed are we as His children to have God's Holy presence live in us through the most precious gift of all, the Holy Ghost!

Thought for the day: If you have not received the gift of the Holy Ghost, today is a great day to receive it!

"Then Peter said unto them, Repent, and be baptized every one of you in the name of Jesus Christ for the remission of sins, and ye shall receive the gift of the Holy Ghost."
(Acts 2:38 – KJV)

MANIFESTATIONS OF GOD'S AGAPE LOVE

You may not be in the best position in life today, in fact you may be facing obstacles, trials and tribulation... but don't let that cause you to be down, depressed or unsettled. Remember everything happens for a reason... nothing takes God by surprise. In fact, what you may see as a setback, or a disappointment, may not be that at all in God's eyes.

Just keep the faith and always remember...This is the day that the Lord hath made, let us rejoice and be glad in it. But as we rejoice and enjoy this beautiful day, let us also watch for God's fingerprints in our lives... for God is so good.

Today could be your day of deliverance, your day of healing, your day of reaching a personal goal, your day of finding that much needed job, or receipt of an answer to prayer you've been waiting for... it could be your day that God does something special. Something so special that He specifically planned just for you! Are you excited to see what He has in store for you today? I know I am.

Thought for the day: Expect to see God perform a miracle in your life today. Watch for it; and then praise God for it.

"Be strong and of a good courage, fear not, nor be afraid of them: for the LORD thy God, he it is that doth go with thee; he will not fail thee, nor forsake thee." (Deut. 31:6 – KJV)

ARE YOU A BRANCH, A LEAF, OR THE TRUNK

I'm thinking about the family tree today. Thinking back on generations from past to present, there may be some people in your family that you are proud to call family, while others may have you feeling a bit embarrassed to be associated with them. Sometimes we allow our roots to determine our status in life. Worse yet, we allow it to hinder our confidence in doing a work for God as we may feel inept or unworthy for God to use us. If you feel that you are not "good enough" to be used by God, think again.

Jesus' family tree had its own flaws. When you read through His family tree you are amazed to see such shady people grace the family tree of the Savior. Between prostitutes, adulterous affairs, and murder just to mention a few, I would say this was definitely a dysfunctional family tree. However, what is truly amazing is that it is, exactly as God designed it. These folks were per-destined and selected by God himself to be a part of this precious family tree of Jesus.

So do not sell yourself short. If you feel like God is reaching out to you to be used for His purpose, let Him. He wants to use you just as you are, regardless of where and how you represent your place in the family tree.

Thought for the day: Look in the mirror today and tell yourself that you are good enough for any task God may call you do. God knows your exact characteristics and flaws, and would not have it any other way. Seek to be used for the Kingdom, you are worth it.

"And if it seem evil unto you to serve the LORD, choose you this day whom ye will serve; whether the gods which your fathers served that were on the other side of the flood, or the gods of the Amorites, in whose land ye dwell: but as for me and my house, we will serve the LORD."
(Jos 24:25 –KJV)

I WAS SENT TO HELP YOU

Sometimes God will leave us in trouble waters; not because he does not care or he wants to see us drown, but to see if we will accept the help he sends us.

God's ways are not our ways, and often he will use the most unlikely people to do His work. Unfortunately, often we will reject them, abuse them, or, simply discard them as insignificant. Then we wonder why we remain in the situations we have found ourselves in.

So many times throughout the Bible we read how God took someone so unsuspecting and used them in such a mighty way that it leaves us in bewilderment.

God may be doing that exact same thing in your life. Just because that person may be younger, not as educated as you are, or even the opposite sex, it does not mean that the spirit of God is not working through them to get to you. Be open-minded to those who may be trying to help you. Pay attention to their words, their countenance, and their love toward you during your difficulties'. If they are trying to help you and not hinder you, they may have been placed in your life to bring about the change you so desperately need.

Often we resist the change necessary especially when it is announced in such a way that we do not want to hear it; or worse, through someone less desirable. Be careful in how you respond. They could very well be an angel in disguise.

Thought for the day: God, please give me the eyes to see what I cannot see clearly... and the humility to accept whom you have entrusted to deliver my rescue.

> *"Iron sharpeneth iron; so a man sharpeneth the countenance of his friend." (Prov. 27:17 – KJV)*

MORNING THOUGHTS

Before my day starts I just want to say thank you. Thank you for waking me up. Thank you for keeping me safe and warm throughout the night. Thank you for allowing me to awake to a sound mind, good health, the ability to walk, talk, hear, see, taste, smell and have all the senses in my body. It is these blessings that you give me that I pray I will never take for granted. I count them as huge blessings that you give me on a daily basis.

As this day unfolds I am asking Lord that you will keep me. Do not permit anything to come into my life that works to separate me from you. Keep me within the palm of your hand, hold onto me, and please just hold me close. Keep my focus on you and the things of the Kingdom. In totality Lord, watch over and keep my soul.

Although I know not your master plan for me this day, help me to recognize it should you choose to reveal it? Help me to see myself through your eyes. Help me acknowledge my weaknesses before you so you can make me strong. Help me worship you in all circumstances that may come my way today. Let me be an encourager to those who need an encouraging word. Let me finish my morning thoughts with these words Lord, "I love you".

Thought for the day: Starting the day with the right mindset can be the difference of the kind of day you may have. Try to begin each new day with morning thoughts of how blessed you are and give thanks to the Lord for those blessings. Who knows, you just might have the best day of your life.

"In every thing give thanks: for this is the will of God in Christ Jesus concerning you."
(I Th. 5:18 KJV)

MAKE IT A SPIRITUAL DAY

Too often we find ourselves pleasing self instead of our spirit. So today, I am challenging us to be pleasers of God.

Take today to live your moments to show the love of Christ to those you meet, removing all evidence of malice and bitterness.

Use today to extend compassion to those who have been perhaps less that compassionate with you. Remember the old saying, "Kill them with kindness."

Line up your life today with the Word of God.

The Word of God was written to assist us in becoming more like Christ. Each word, sentence, paragraph holds insight, wisdom, direction, guidance and yes even judgment.

Today, pick a verse out of the Bible and live it to the fullest. If you choose a verse you are unsure of what the insight, wisdom, direction, guidance or judgment may be outlining, pray over it. Ask God to speak the meaning of the scripture into your life.

If you choose a verse that you are aware of what God is speaking through the words, at the end of the day assess how well you lined up with God's desired outcome.

Thought for the day: Seek to be more spiritual today than carnal.

"This I say then, Walk in the Spirit, and ye shall not fulfil the lust of the flesh." (Gal. 5:16 – KJV)

LIFE TO REMEMBER

Yesterday is gone. There is nothing you can do to change the choices you made, the wrongs you did, or even enhance the good deeds you have done. It is in the history book.

Tomorrow is still in the making. It has not arrived yet. Although you have been taught it is good to have a plan for the future, you must not live in the future, because none are promised to see tomorrow.

Then you have today. What you do today will determine what will be written in the history book about you? The question is when the history book is opened, and your name is spoken, what will it say.

Will your name, your life be remembered as a legacy of hope, faith and love? Or perhaps it will tell of all of your worldly accomplishments and the fortune you left behind to your children or to charity. There is yet another way you may be remembered and that may be in a less favorable manner. The beauty of writing your history is you are the author of it. You decide.

There are some choices in your life that may be the product of obligations, compromise or even out of your control. Should these circumstances affect your life; how you address these adversities will be a big part of your remembrance. Think before you react, listen before you speak, and be careful how you treat others, as your history is being written daily. So happy writing.

Thought for the day: You are in control of how you are remembered; make sure you are remembered favorably.

"Let your light so shine before men, that they may see your good works, and glorify your Father which is in heaven."
(Matt 5:16 – KJV)

MY SON... THE SAILOR

As you set out to defend our country,
Remember what I raised you to be.
A man of love, honor and integrity,
A man of God, as you set sea.

Don't forget to pray each day,
For the Lord to have his way.
Although you must yield to your earthly boss,
Don't sell your soul for any cost.

As you serve your country in the Armed Forces
out on the open sea,
I must accept you are where you want to be.
Be safe; don't take needless chances with your life
I plead,
Just come home ~ Come back to me.

Often as parents we want to shield our children from the ugliness of the world. However, our children make choices for themselves which may lead them right into harm's way. We must always remember to allow them the freedom of choice, but equip them with the power to keep them. That power? The Word of God! The Power of God! The Faith in God! The Will of God! When we have done this, we have done our part and the rest is up to them and God.

Thought for the day: It is never easy letting go of our children and loved one to a called service that may cost them their life. In times when you are feeling lonely, scared or even desperate, remember that you have instilled in them the tools necessary to be successful in life. Today, say an extra prayer for him or her and ask God to keep them in his hand wherever they may be. Ask God to give you a sign that your loved one is safe and believe that he will.

"Train up a child in the way he should go: and when he is old, he will not depart from it." (Proverbs 22:6 – KJV)

I HAVE A FRIEND

I have a friend, a very special friend and his name is JESUS.

He made the trees, and he made the seas, he even made the bubble bees, his name is JESUS.

J-E-S-U-S but it all together and what do you get, you get JESUS!

I have a friend, a very special friend and his name is JESUS.

He made the moon, and he made the sun, he even made everyone, his name is JESUS.

J-E-S-U-S but is all together and what do you get, you get JESUS.

How awesome is it to know you have a friend in Jesus. That the Creator of the world, not only knows you but he personally designed you!

Thought for the day: If you are feeling all alone today, remember that you have a friend that is always with you. Why not tell him your troubles and let him soothe you. After all he knows you better than anyone else.

"But even the very hairs of your head are all numbered. Fear not therefore: ye are of more value than many sparrows."
(Luke 12:7 – KJV)

A MOTHER'S LOVE

I felt you move within me, fight to be free,

Free to enter this world, free to just Be.

I watched you grow from twenty inches to several feet tall,

And helped you rollover and urged you to crawl.

I clapped when you uttered your first word,

And cried at your first step.

I smiled at your curiosity at seeing a bird,

And stood in awe as you slept.

That was many years ago, when I tickled your toes,

But yet it seems like yesterday that we ran, jumped and played

in the snow.

I felt your fear as we walked to school, the look in your eyes

asking,

"Mommy what should I do?"

I helped you with your ABC's,

and then you showed me your 123's.

I encouraged you to be the best you could be,

And hid my disappointment when you brought home a D.

Oh that seems so very long ago,

When I was mom, the mom in the "know".

Now I'm mom who doesn't understand,

The mom marching to a different band.

Oh Motherhood thru the years,

We calm their fears, wipe away their tears.

We see their good, their bad, the ugly it's true,

But Mother's keep loving, no matter what they do.

God gave us the blessing to give birth,

And the curse to have our emotions trampled on, as common dirt.

Motherhood, blessing or Curse, I wouldn't change a thing,

And that's what makes it worse,

God knew what he was doing,

When he gave the gift from above,

Because there's nothing like, a Mother's Love.

"A woman when she is in travail hath sorrow, because her hour is come: but as soon as she is delivered of the child, she remembereth no more the anguish, for joy that a man is born into the world." (John 16:21 – KJV)

THINKING OUT LOUD QUOTES

1. Surrender... no one wants to do it, but sometimes surrendering is the action that is required by God in order for Him to give you victory.

2. I wish for just one day... everyone would get along, everyone would speak a blessing to others, and unconditional love was the norm and not a rarity.

3. I will continue to inspire even if you are uninspired. I will continue to encourage even if you are not encouraged. I will continue to love even if your actions are unlovable... bottom line... I will continue to be a Christian even if you don't want me to be... because it's who I am and you will not defeat me.

4. There comes a time when the only opinion that you worry about is God's.

5. It amazes me that other people can live my life better than I can.

6. When all else fails, pray; and when you feel like that isn't working, pray harder.

7. God is molding me into perfection; I never said I was there yet.

8. Thinking positive is no longer the norm, so dare to be different.

9. You are in control of your emotions don't give that power to others.

10. When the opportunity arises to show love, do it. It may be a test from God.

11. No matter what be a person of integrity.

12. It is easy to have faith when everything is going right; but real faith is believing in the worst of times.

13. They call it women's intuition; I call it a lie detector.

14. I want to see you through loving eyes, not through natural eyes.

15. We have all that we need in Jesus.

16. You ask, "Why won't you bless me God"... and God says " I did... it is standing right in front of you, but you refuse to see it."

17. Do not let fear and doubt take up residency in your heart. When they knock, let faith and confidence take over.

CPSIA information can be obtained
at www.ICGtesting.com
Printed in the USA
FFOW01n1152180315
11900FF